My Pirate Ship

Captain Greybeard and his crew invite aboard:

....

Write your pirate name here

priddy books

Welcome Aboard

Ahoy, matey! Welcome aboard the Jolly Roger,
the best pirate ship on the seven seas!

Captain Greybeard

This is Captain Greybeard!
He sails the Jolly Roger
and takes the crew on lots
of exciting adventures.
Can you find his favourite
golden sword among
the stickers?

First Mate, Polly Silvers

Polly Silvers is Captain Greybeard's
second in command. She is quicker
with a cutlass than anyone else on
the Jolly Roger!

Master of Cannons, Bill Blast

Bill Blast makes sure
the gun deck is kept
shipshape! Can you
stick colourful patches
on his clothes?

Help the crew get ready to set sail by colouring in their costumes and using your stickers to complete their pirate kit!

Patch and Buckle

Patch and Buckle are pirates-in-training. They have lots of chores to do, but always manage to find plenty of time for mischief with Boots the dog.

Chef, Mr Pots

Mr Pots is the Jolly Roger's cook. He makes hearty meals for all the crew. Can you find his parrot, Pepper?

Lookout, Sharp-Eyed Sam

Sharp-Eyed Sam sits in the crow's nest and reports anything he sees through his trusty telescope. Can you find his cat, Ruby?

The Ship

It's time to find your sea legs.
Let's explore the Jolly Roger!

The Gun Deck

The Crew's Quarters

The Ship's Jail

Colour in the rooms on each deck and add stickers.
Can you find Patch and Buckle's secret den?

Psst! Here is Patch and Buckle's den.
Fill it with pirate goodies!

The Captain's Cabin

The Galley

The Hold

The Main Deck

Captain Greybeard summons his crew.
"All hands, on deck!"

Fill the scene with busy pirates swabbing
the decks, reading maps and firing cannons!

The Crow's Nest

Up in the crow's nest, Sharp-Eyed Sam keeps watch.
What can he see through his telescope?

SAM'S
MAPS

Fill the scene with sea creatures, ships and seabirds.
Where is Sharp-Eyed Sam's compass?

The Captain's Cabin

Captain Greybeard's cabin is full of booty
he has collected on his travels.

Colour in his favourite things and use your
stickers to fill the cabin with more of his pirate swag!

The Crew's Quarters

In the crew's quarters, the pirates
take a break after a long day.

PIRATE
GAMES

Use colours and stickers to make this room
fit for a swashbuckling pirate crew!

The Gun Deck

There she blows! Bill Blast and his assistants,
Spark and Flint, are testing the cannons.

Fill the deck with ammunition.
Don't forget to colour in the cannons!

The Galley

Mr Pots is cooking a hearty meal for the crew,
while Patch and Buckle bake some yummy cakes!

Fill the room with delicious pirate grub!
What is Polly having for dinner?

The Ship's Jail

Shiver me timbers! It looks like someone
has escaped the Jolly Roger's jail!

Find the buccaneer and put him back behind bars!
Can you find a padlock to make the jail secure?

The Hold

Down in the hold, the crew stores all the treasure they find on their adventures!

Use your stickers to fill the hold full of
silver daggers, glittering gold and sparkling jewels!

Under the Sea

Man overboard! The crew is searching
an old shipwreck for hidden treasure.

**Fill the page with colourful sea creatures,
swimming shipmates and lots of treasure
for the pirates to find!**

Treasure Map

Patch has found a treasure map hidden in a bottle!
Colour in the map and draw a cross to mark
where the treasure is!

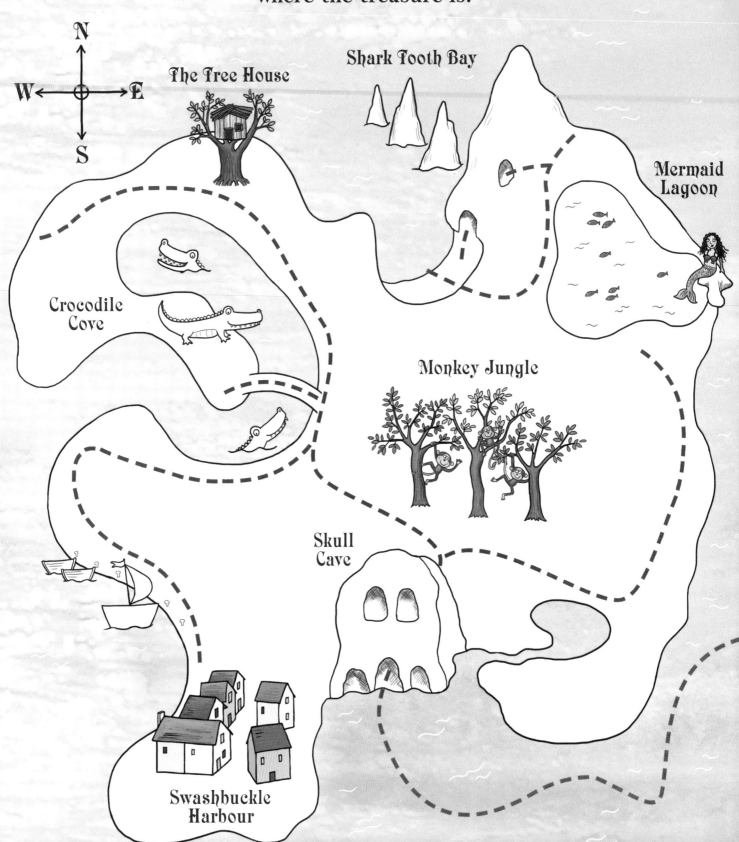

N
W E
S

The Tree House

Shark Tooth Bay

Mermaid Lagoon

Crocodile Cove

Monkey Jungle

Skull Cave

Swashbuckle Harbour

Welcome Aboard

The Ship

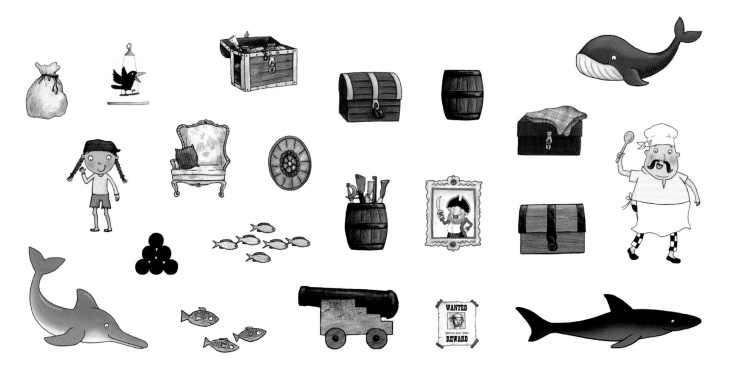

The Main Deck

The Crow's Nest

The Captain's Cabin

The Crew's Quarters

The Gun Deck

The Galley

The Ship's Jail

The Hold

Under the Sea